A Christmas Story

MAN IN HIS ELEMENT:

OR,

A NEW WAY TO KEEP HOUSE.

Dr. Samuel W. Francis

[ZHINGOORA BOOKS]

CONTENTS

PART I.

A WOMAN'S PLAN.

'My dear Mary,' said I, one morning, to my widowed sister, as she sank into an arm chair in front of my library fire, and heaved a sigh replete with exhaustion and sadness:

'What is the matter?'

'Enough for a woman, William, but of course, nothing for an old bachelor like you, who have only to pay your own bills, eat your meals without the trouble of ordering them; lounge through a clean house with no chasing after servants to sweep and wash and dust; sit in your study, heaping log after log on your devoted andirons, and always meeting me with such a provoking cheerfulness, while I have not a moment to myself; am all the time running to give out stores to one girl; soap and starch to another; candles and linen to the chambermaid, and orders to the coachman; and, even then, I have no peace; for, no sooner do I sit in the nursery, hoping to derive a few minutes comfort from a quiet sew, than my ears are filled with the dissatisfaction of one girl; the complaints of another; the threatenings to leave of another, and the quarrels of all. I declare, William, I think it was too bad in you to insist on our leaving that comfortable boarding house, where we lived so much cheaper, and had no trouble. It was there, with my small family, that I appreciated the freedom from care that you old selfish, unsympathizing bachelors enjoy; and no wonder you laugh at us. The fact is, you don't know anything about it; you ——'

'My dear Mary,' I repeated, 'you have said enough—I only ask for a few minutes to put this matter in a new light, and, in time, you yourself will be convinced.'

[4]

'That's all very well, William, but what's the use of talking to you men. I never convinced one in my life. No sir! man is an animal that never acknowledges either that he is wrong, or that a woman is right. I tell you, servants are the bane of my existence. You cannot make them happy, do what you may. Why, only the other day I gave Jane a nice pair of gaiters that I had but partially worn out. She thanked me, and I felt pleased that I had done one kind action, though it was a self-denial. The very next morning, in coming out of the kitchen, I passed the ash barrel, and looked in it to see if the cinders would ever be sifted. What do you suppose I saw there, mixed up with lemon peel, tea leaves and ashes? My boots, William—the very pair I had given Jane the day before.'

'Well what did you do?'

'Do? Why as soon as I could recover I called her to me, and asked why she had[Pg 2] thrown them there.' She said without any excitement, that was the worst of it, 'I couldn't wear them Madam.'

'Why not?' I said.

'They were too large for me.'

'Too large for her, the jade—think of that'—

'Don't say any more, Mary, I understand the case perfectly—and since we cannot argue upon the matter just listen to my views (without any interruption), in the form of a philosophical lecture. It will be very brief but to the point.

'Though I have never kept house, as I am an old man I must have lived somewhere all my life. Being possessed of a healthy and observing intellect—I have seen and digested much; and it is all easy to my mind. I have heard you through as I have heard others through; I have seen your sufferings and your trials, as I have seen many, very many suffer and endure trials, and I have solved the problem and told it all to my segar!'

[5]

'Well now that is selfish, William!'

'Not at all my dear sister, what lady would tolerate the slightest interference with her housekeeping? How long would you permit me to stay here, in financial partnership, if I even offered one word of advice.'

'Oh, how unjust, speak out now and let me hear what you have confided to your segar.'

'Well, in the first place, there are two kinds of ways to keep house. No. one is to keep your servants; No. two is to be kept by them. Herein is the key note of much trouble. Another difficulty is fear. I have been perfectly amazed to listen to ladies when asking a waiter to do something for them. Just think of it. I heard Mrs. ——, at table the other day, turn round and look towards a red headed, uplifted girl, with a conciliatory smile and say, 'Betty, would you mind giving me a glass of water?'

'Zounds madam, I wanted to scream!—and only last night, while paying a visit I heard a lady who rules her elegant husband to within an inch of his life, say to the waiter, 'John, please put on your things and muffle up well, for it is very cold and do take this note to Mrs. Henry's' and, almost with the same breath, she turned on her husband and said, 'Albert, go down and get that medicine *at once* for you know I cannot retire till I take it—you can see *your* friend any time,' looking at me in a hard manner and then at the clock. 'Now what do you call that? That woman has courage to meet her equals and put all things straight; but a menial crushes her.'

'Well, of course you don't understand those things, William, but I do.'

'I suppose so, but I don't want to. It is all wrong—all *humbug*, all trash!' I exclaimed as my excitement knocked the ashes of my segar over my clean shirt.

[6]

'What would you have us do?' exclaimed Mary, a little nettled at my last remark.

'Do?' I replied, with emphasis; 'let the men keep house. Watch them, and learn the true method, which has for its motto,

"Maximum of work,

Minimum of trouble."'

By this time I began to feel anxious.—My sister had gone off into a fit of laughter[Pg 3] that at first greatly roused my ire, but ultimately awakened anxiety, for she could not gain her breath. I rang for a servant; of course none came, for she always had to call them. 'They were having such a good time down stairs, they could not hear the bell,' so I poured out a glass of water, and, while she drank, seized the poker; stirred up the dying embers; put on a good back log; lit a large and strong Cabana to lend zest to my courage, and prepared to make one more effort for victory.

Gradually subsiding into a few occasional chromatic giggles, Mary looked through her beautiful eyes, glistening with tears of fun, and said, in a smothered whisper,

'Well, and what would you do?'

'Do?' I repeated. 'Let me have the reins for one month, and I will show you.'

There! it was out, and I felt relieved.

'But, William,' she whispered, pointing with anxiety to the door which stood ajar, 'how long do you suppose they would stay with you?'

'Until they got married or died!' I answered with confidence, and, sitting bolt upright, I ran both thumbs under my waistcoat arm-holes and played on my chest with my fingers, while I puffed tremendously to envelope my countenance with smoke, the better to hide my ill-concealed smile.

'You single men are too amusing, my dear brother,' said she, looking earnestly into my face and patting my shoulder with an expression of pity. 'To convince you that woman's mission is the care of domestic matters; and, as I would like a little rest combined with fun, I will turn over everything to you, and——'

'Done!' I yelled with delight, and jumping up, I paced up and down the library like a prisoner freed from chains.—'Done! Oh! I thank you, Mary.'

'Stop, young man,' she said, with assumed severity, 'hear the conditions of the bond.'

'Write it down,' I said, in haste, 'and so long as I am to have the reins I will sign.'

'Well, sir,' said she, entering with her old accustomed gaiety into the subject matter. 'I agree to let you keep house on the following conditions:' naming a good many, which I listened to with marked interest, and finally condensed into the form of a written contract, though no lawyer; for fear, as I told her, she would violate the premises. As well as I can remember, for it was many years ago—it ran as follows:

'This agreement made this 24th November, 1853, between Mary Walters of the city, county and state of New York, being party of the first part, and William d'Aubrey of the said city, county and state of New York, party of the second part, witnesseth as follows: Said party of the first part agrees, covenants and binds herself, heirs and assinines—I mean assigns—to surrender, demise and make over all claim, right and title to housekeeping, and all matters pertaining to the welfare of household economy, whether trivial or special, to the party of the second part; moreover delivering up all accounts, keys and inventory of stores now on hand, and all claim, right or title to the management of each and every person living, or about to live in premises known as 'Villa Felice,' [Pg 4]situated at the outskirts of the city of —— in the State of ——, for the period of three months. Now, in consideration of this obligation on the party of the first part, the party of the second part covenants, agrees and binds himself, his heirs and assinines—I mean assigns—to act conscientiously for the benefit of all the inhabitants of said 'Villa Felice,' whether male or female;—and moreover pledges himself never by word or deed to consult, ask questions of, molest by interrogated words, or lead on by indirect remarks, the party of the first part; to impart, give over or yield up, any information on or concerning the subject or principle of housekeeping—(this last clause my sister insisted on in a most impressive manner—so I added the following,) and it is distinctly understood, comprehended by, and agreed to between both parties, that the party of the first part interferes with, molests, makes the subject of remark, indirectly or directly, impugns or maligns, the party of the second party in the pursuit of lawful proceedings neither by appeal, nor by entreaty, nor by satire, irony, libel, gossip, hinted evidence or such other expressions of mental feeling which are unseemly and tend to weaken man's power or involve in confusion a settled purpose. Said agreement to take effect at once on the signing of this contract,' made in duplicate.

Signed, sealed and delivered the afore-written day, month and year, in the presence of

Witness,
MARY WALTERS, [seal.]
WILLIAM D'AUBREY, [seal.]

We both signed, and then remembered a witness was necessary. 'I will call Thomas,' said Mary. 'He won't know what we have written.' I bowed with a legal stiffness, and waited. She rang—no response.

She rang again. A loud laughter in the kitchen caused her to say, as usual, 'Oh! they cannot hear the bell,' and she tripped off lightly and called 'Susan! Susan! *Susan!*' 'and but the booming roars replied and fast the talk rolled on.' 'Susan,' said she, gently, over the bannisters.

'Susan is out, marm,' said a granite voice from the second story.

'Don't speak so loud, marm. Johnny has just gone to sleep, and I've had such trouble with him all the evening; he must have caught cold going to dancing school. You know, marm I begged you not to send him.

'Mrs. Phillips,' whispered Mary, in a crushed voice, 'where has Susan gone?'

'She went to her sister's, marm. Her child is very ill with the small pox, and she said she knew, if you knew he might die, that you would let her go and sit up with him this last night, poor, dear soul, bless his heart!'

Oh, how I chuckled!

'Why, Mrs. Phillips, just come down stairs, please; I want to speak to you.—Come into the library, only Mr. D'Aubrey is here.'

(Humph! Only Mr. D'Aubrey!—'Oh, for to-morrow!')

Enter Mrs. Phillips, one of those fat, pylygastric nurses, who divide the twenty-four hours into four days, so as to have three meals to each of their diurnal revolutions; whose digestive organs, if they could speak, would strike for wages; whose eyes move but never look; their atmosphere[Pg 5]—what Germans might call expression—being that of massive rest.

She slides into the room and immediately sits down, moving her eyes up to her mistress with a patient and slightly suffering expression, while the process of deglutition is slowly going on.

I seize a book, pamphlet, anything, hold it in front of my face, and bite my segar in two.

'Did I understand you to say, Mrs. Phillips, that Susan had gone to sit up with a *small pox* patient?'

'Her nephew, yes marm.'

'Oh, how very wrong in her—how—'

'I don't think so, marm.'

I ground my teeth.

'Why Mrs. Phillips?'

'The boy marm, may not be yours, but it is her *kin* and she ought to know her duty to a sister's child.'

'Yes, but she might bring the disease to my little children! she'—
'That's in the hands of Providence, marm.'

I ram a handkerchief down my mouth and choke—

'Well, as it is not your fault I need not speak to you—but please be so kind as to call Thomas, I only want him for a moment.' The celebrated Mrs. Phillips heaved a sigh, pregnant with bread, butter, cold meat and ale; and slid out of the room, crunching her way down stairs. I peeped at my sister—she looked pale and very anxiously perplexed, I pinched myself and kept silent. In a few minutes a voice was heard singing up the back stairs and—enter Sabina spread out with starch and heavily pomaded hair. 'Mrs. Phillips sent me to tell you marm that she had to make her gruel and the fire was low—and that Thomas had gone home.'

'Why, what time is it, Sabina?'

[11]

'*Eight* o'clock,' I enunciate distinctly. For one moment Mary's eyes lit up with something like heroism, but before she could frame a sentence, the playful want of interest exhibited by Sabina, who leaned against the mantel-piece, straightening her cuffs, did the business, and she collapsed.

'Please tell Thomas, when he comes to-morrow, Sabina, I would rather not have him go home quite as early, because you see,' (oh how I mentally groaned at this humiliating nonsense,) 'I might want him. You won't forget, will you, Sabina?'

'No, marm. Is there anything else?' Having now made herself prim, and taken a quiet survey of the library and viewed me carefully, she was now desirous of retiring.

'One moment, Sabina,' said Mary, beginning to realize her false position before me, 'Who is down stairs?'

'Well, I couldn't tell you, marm.'

'Why not?'

'There are so many.'

'How, do you mean so many?'

'Why, marm, it's the cook's birthday; and she thought you would'nt mind her having a few friends, so she invited her *cousins*,' (looking at me as though she would ask, 'what have you got to say to that, Mr. Man?')

'Well, Sabina,' said Mary, coloring up in confusion, 'just sign your name to this—it is only as a witness.'

'I cannot write, marm,' answered dandy Amazon, very short at being exposed.[Pg 6]

'Then send Elizabeth here.'

'She is out too, marm.'

'What? Elizabeth has gone out?'

'Yes marm, you see,' (becoming confidential,) 'the cook and her has quarrelled like—she neglected to ask her to her little party till late this evening, and so she got huffy and put on her things and dashed out of the house,' (at this time I had either an attack of the ague or was laughing so hard internally that it leaked through.)

'Is Dinah in?'

'Yes marm.'

'Ask her, please, to come here.'

Sabina tripped off with a satisfied air, and five—ten—fifteen minutes elapsed and no Ellen. I took out my memorandum and quickly wrote down a few valuable plans on the coming campaign. The clock struck half past eight, and my sister opened the entry door and listened—the kitchen door soon shut and somebody came up stairs slowly, with a waiter full of something.

'Is that you, Dinah?'

'Yes marm.'

'Why didn't you come before?'

'I don't know, mum.'

'Didn't Sabina tell you I wanted you?'

'No, mum. She told me you wanted to know how many were down stairs, and I counted seventeen.'

[13]

'Take care Dinah, you're spilling that milk!'

'I can't help it, this pitcher leaks.'

'Where's the children's bowl?'

'I don't know, mum—I think it's broke.'

'Broken! Why, I bought a new one yesterday.'

"Tain't my fault.'

Hopelessly resigned, my sister Mary politely requested her to put down the waiter, and explained the nature of a witness's duty. We acknowledged our signatures and Dinah wrote out her name in a neat hand, then picked up the waiter and walked out of the room with the air of an injured innocent.

I jumped up, kissed my sister, informed her that for the next three months she was to be a *passive* observer, asked her to retire, locked up the contract, and gave the bell one pull that brought half the household to the door.

PART II.

A MAN'S PLAN.

As the servants rushed into the library they found me quietly reading a book and puffing at the pages. I slightly raised my eyes to this back ground of faces on which might be seen, surprise, anger, impertinence, curiosity and excitement. I slowly placed my book half open across my knee, with my hand resting on the cover, and with the other taking my segar out of my mouth, knocked the ashes off into a little glass tub; elevated my eyebrows and asked in perfect astonishment, yet measured tones:

'What-is-the-matter?'

'That's what we want to know sir;' exclaimed the cook, a little let down by my coolness.

'Nothing that I know of,' I replied, except that I took the liberty of ringing my bell,' increasing in volume as I spoke.

'We thought some one was sick, sir,' said Sabina.

'I don't want to know what *you* thought,' I rolled out in emphatic base, 'I want the[Pg 7] waiter! which is *it*?'—That neuter cut them to the heart.

But they rallied—a revolt was imminent. I had lived in the family one year, with my sister as housekeeper, and had never made a remark to the servants, it being my habit in life to submit to what was not my business, or clear out. But now—*now*, with Imprimatur on my forehead, a clutch in my mental fingers, and a hungry longing to rule free: ha! ha!—Let us see. This was a trying moment—The vessel had been signalled, and my colors were to be shown—so here they go—the flag of the little brig 'one-man-power,' with the motto 'Anvil or hammar answer hammar,' is unfurled.

[15]

Hemmed in by swelling indignation, whisperings and sullen looks, I jumped up and yelled in stentorian voice:

'Leave my room! How dare you answer the waiter's bell? Send me the waiter and clear out, every one of you!' and, with a sweeping wave of my hand, I stalked towards the door. Reader, did you ever see the sun chase a big cloud right off a green field, and, with no respite, drive it headlong away over beyond the horizon? Such was the rapid departure of my stupefied retainers. On reaching the door, I slammed it to with a violence that echoed through the hushed and palsied house.

Oh the benefit of a good slam—not a push—nor a quick shut—nor even a bump, all of which show still a want of firmness and decision—but a good old-fashioned 'bang' as though it had got into your throat and you could'nt breathe—that life depended on shutting out a flash of lightning and you hadn't time to wait—that the harder you impelled it against the doorway the sooner would end fast fleeting agony—that the nearer you got to what might be called an *explosive shut*: the more complete would be your safety, that if all your concentrated passion could be, not flung, (that is too weak) but hurled at that one partition a vacuum might be made in your room towards which good impulses might be drawn inversely. Many a good natured man who has been cornered by injustice has slammed off his anger, and is ready to forgive, but not give up. There is a dignity in this rapid developement of muscular power which admits of no surrender—the gauntlet has been thrown down, the chip has been knocked off the shoulder, the black flag is hoisted and skull and bones stand out in bold relief. There may be a calm, the wind may die out, but the monster waves once lashed up to a Titanic power move on of their own accord, and wash away the very vestige of resistance. Asking to *be* forgiven after slamming a door is like touching off a Rodman gun, and then calling out to the fort in front to 'look out' 'take care!' 'do get out of the way.' A first class slam is cumulative long after the noise has ceased—the nerves go on slamming—the valves of the heart flap to and from—the tympanum roils a revelrie to all the shattered senses, the offender slammed at, at once subsides from rage to fear; the mental barometer falls—and

[16]

apprehension—the requiescat—is a don't know what is coming next. A bona fide, abandoned slam is a Domestic Earthquake.

I next sat down on my Mexican chair, and waited for the rapid hatching of the egg. A register led up from the kitchen[Pg 8] into my room, and though never used, formed one of those abominable listening tubes that might be truthfully called family tale-bearers. This time, however, I had the pleasure of overhearing the following fragmentary evidence of a reaction:

'He must be crazy.' 'Did he drink much after dinner?' 'I say, you have been here longer than I have, have you ever seen him so before?' Then a giggle, and some one saying: 'Is he married?'

'Sabina, ain't you ashamed to laugh?'—'poor thing—won't stay—gallows'—then silence, and in a few minutes one after another of the visitors passed by under the window on tip-toe, and almost immediately a soft knock and a pause. I thought * * * and acted.

'Come in,' said I, in one of those gentle and subdued voices that no one but a passionate man can possess. The door gradually opened, and there stood Susan, the devoted aunt.

I had placed a volume of engravings before my eyes, and was busily engaged in drawing some plan, on paper, as she entered. I went on for a little while in silence, when she said:

'I understood, sir——'

I said 'wait a minute,' and went on ruling one entire side, with double lines, in perfect forgetfulness of her presence.

When she spoke again, 'Did you send for me, sir?' I would have answered at once, for I felt awfully at appearing such a tyro; but the case was a desperate one of long standing, and required heroic treatment. I kept her waiting, at first as a lesson, that her imagination might take wings and fly to the uttermost realms of unhappiness. The

[17]

second time, I thought I detected a little impatience in her voice, so I said, taking a pen and dipping it in red ink, 'wait one moment, Susan,' and went on lining and interlining. This was not reading, studying, nor writing; it was what she very well knew I could do any time. So it told on her. Each moment her valor oozed out, and as soon as I felt that the cup of bitterness was pretty well drained, I proceeded to offer up this victim as a sacrifice to peace.

'Susan, how is your sister's child?'

I looked straight into her. There was no sternness or smartness in my expression, but the gaze was mathematical. I was measuring her candor, and analyzing her mind.

She colored up and said, 'he's no better, sir; and they've given him up: but the doctor says good nursing will do wonders.'

'I think so, too. Go back to your sister and stay till he is better; I will supply your place.'

This puzzled her, but she could say nothing. I meant 'go' and she went.—There was no delay—I saw her walk by the window almost at once, and overheard the whisper, 'who next?'

I now rang the bell, and Dinah came to the door, saying, before she knocked, the waiter is out, sir, so I answered your ring.

'Do you know where Thomas lives?'

'Yes sir.'

'Then tell him I want him now—'

'Yes sir,' she disappeared.

Oh the benefit of that *slam*.

[18]

In half an hour in walked Thomas.

'Never do you enter my room without knocking. It is a piece of impertinence I will not put up with.'[Pg 9]

'I did not mean anything by it, sir.'

'Well, don't do it again, and always take your hat off when you come before a gentleman or lady. Such ignorance might lose you a good place.'

His wages were high I knew. It was also winter, and he gave in. He stood still with his hat in hand and waited.

'Thomas I want you to bring the close carriage to the door with the two bays.'

'Yes sir; but the off horse cast his hind shoe yesterday and I am afraid.'

'You need not be, the ground is covered with snow. I shall want the carriage in fifteen minutes.'

'Yes sir, but—'

'But what?'

'I left the carriage this morning at the blacksmiths to have a new tire put on it, sir.'

'Who told you to?'

'Nobody, sir.'

'Then never do anything of that kind again without first reporting it to me.'

[19]

'Yes sir,' moving slightly towards the door as though it was all settled now.

'What other vehicle have you got in the stable?'

'The Phæton, sir; the open box wagon and the carryall.'

'Very well then, bring the nigh horse round in the carryall.'

'He never went in single harness since I drove Mrs. ——'

'Well, then, put the other one in.'

'Nor him neither, sir.'

'Humph!' it looked a little black.

'Well, where is the other horse, the gray, that your mistress always drives when alone?'

'He is at the veterinary surgeons, sir.—I took him there last Monday and he is to be blistered for two weeks off and on, sir.'

'Well, Thomas, as the coachman of the family, I ask you what can be done.

'I *must* go out to-night. Can you suggest anything?'

'Nothing but to hire a hack, sir.'

'That's a very good idea, how far is the livery stable from here?'

'Just next to where I live, sir. I can get one in a minute, sir.'

Oh! so cheerfully.

'Very well, Thomas, just harness the two bays and ride down there and put them to one. Tell the livery stable keeper that I wish it, and will pay for the use of it.'

'But, sir, it is——'

'Thomas, I would advise you not to be long. You ought to be ashamed to call yourself a coachman, and have what is under your charge in such a condition. The idea of a horse two days without a shoe.'

'It isn't my——'

'Not a word—go and do your duty in future. I shall expect you here in half an hour.'

He backed out of the room, longing to say something (what it was I don't care) but completely at sea. As he passed under my window, (though I have not sworn for many years,) I am pretty sure I heard several full sized oaths. At the appointed time the bell rang and I went out and got into the carriage. The horses looked very warm, and, though the night was cold, one was covered with foam. I said nothing, but told him to drive to Susan's sister's.

On arriving at the door, I heard sounds of very lively music for a dying child, and saw the house all lighted up.[Pg 10]

'Oh, I understand, it is one of those Hibernian wakes. Poor thing!' and I began to pardon Susan, feel sorry for the coachman, and made up my mind to give $10 towards the sepulchral expenses. As I entered the house, surcharged with benevolence and overcome by a repentant feeling, I caught sight of Susan and a strapping man whirling round the floor to the tune of the Irish Washwoman. I approached her and said, 'I hope he is better.' She uttered a scream and ran out of the room.

The next morning after having gone over everything in the house, I sent for each servant and told them quietly but firmly that my sister's health was not very good, and that I was housekeeper—that as they had engaged to fill certain positions, I should take it for granted they understood their business; that I had neither the time nor would I take the trouble to overlook their work, but that as soon as I saw anything wrong they would hear from me. If they wanted anything I was the person. My housekeeping hours were from 9 till 10 a. m., no more. If they could not take the trouble to ask for what they wanted at that time, they could go without till the next day. I should not tell them what to do or when to do it, but if it wasn't done, they would certainly leave. That I allowed no company and gave them certain nights to go out, but if anything special and *true* was the matter I was ready to assist, 'and now,' said I, 'no quarreling down stairs; each one to their work and no complaining.—The moment you are discontented come to me and you can go at once if you choose. I do not want any notice ever, except where a baby is concerned.' This done I then advertised for a cook. The next day my cook, down stair, came up to me quite flushed, and wanted to know if I intended to turn her away. I said no, I had no idea of it, but thought it was a very good plan to have two in the house; that I intended making the new one a waiter, and then if anything happened, such as the sudden departure, 'of my cook,' I said, looking right at her, 'for you know they are quick tempered, why then I have one on hand.' She colored up and retired. After going through a great deal of nonsense about the words 'help' and 'servants,' I at length got what I wanted and all went on smoothly for a time.

My plan for detecting neglect in the cleaning of a room, was to stick half a dozen pins in different places about it—some on the walls, in the window and other places that ought to be wiped. If I found them there after the cleaning, I became suddenly very disagreeable.

During my sister's administration, I had been obliged to wait sometimes three weeks before she could find time, for her servants, to put a button on my waistcoat. Now, when I wanted anything done, the first person that passed my library door was stopped, no matter what her work might be at the time, sent for a clothes brush, needle

[22]

or hammar, and the thing was done at once. It acted like a charm, and all went on well. At first they objected, (only silently), but I told them plainly that I hired them for my benefit, not theirs, which generally followed; and that though their work was specified to a certain degree, they must on all occasions answer any calls and pay always for breakage. This last saved twenty dollars a month, for hardly anything under those expensive circumstances, fell[Pg 11] of their hands; and I noticed the plea of 'sudden change of weather,' or 'some one must have disturbed it,' or 'that horrid cat has been among those dishes and upset them,' or 'twas cracked before,' became as worn out as aphorisms of the past. I was always very attentive to them when sick. This tells, in the long run, on servants, for they are very susceptible to a kind act out of place—indulgence, however, is soon forgotten. I always made it a habit, too, to pay each servant something more a month than any one else. That, also, acted wonderfully like a retainer. But I distinctly told them I wanted my work done, because it was paid for. I asked no favors. Two other rules saved me much trouble. When a girl said she couldn't do any set job, on account of no time, no matter what it was, I always said, 'why, that's all nonsense; it only takes five minutes;' and not infrequently have I irritated them into doing almost impossibilities. I never valued any cheap article under five dollars.

Another great mistake, is to find fault with a servant before any one. Have they done wrong, go to your library and ring loudly—that is half the battle; then tell the waiter to call the chambermaid, and then speak. You will find everything easy. They have had time to reflect; to weigh the pros and cons, and have half thought themselves into submission. Never argue. If you have the right exert it, but never be unjust; and, above all, believe me when I tell you that their feelings are exquisite on the subject of neglect. Let them once feel a *respect* for you, yet know you are determined to have anything done, and a simple remark will lie like lead on their stomach, and you will hear them talking of it down stairs and using the bow anchor of firmness, 'he said so,' until it is done. Never change your mind.

I remember once, during that memorable interregnum of three months, and, in fact, the only time in my life did it happen.—I had invited some very pleasant, agreeable and talented friends to spend the evening. I ordered my supper in the morning, and it commenced to snow. I continued giving orders, and it continued snowing, and we kept at it very close on to each other; if anything, the snow was a little ahead, but I went on in the same way. At the proposed time the gas was lit, a lantern was placed on the piazza; snow swept off; the side gate unhung by the waiter man, and a path made. The snow piled high, and the domestics began to give in, or out, I don't know which. They doubted the probability of any one venturing out that 'dreadful night.' A little later, they began to talk among themselves of the improbability of any one coming. I immediately ordered the gas turned up in full; the candles lit, and the supper table laid—every dish put in its place empty, to be filled at the proper time—all for discipline. (I had said it was to be done in the morning.) I then went up stairs and dressed. My sister, who had gained five pounds every week since her abdication, met me in the drawing room, dressed elegantly, and with an encouraging air pressed my hand. She did not dare to make a remark, or the contract would have been violated; but I thought I could detect in her eye an acknowledgment of my success. As I sauntered through the brilliantly lighted rooms, rather depressed at[Pg 12] the non-arrival of my guests, the waiter said Thomas would like to speak to me. I immediately went to the star chamber and took an easy position.

A knock this time.

'Come in.'

In walked Thomas with his hat in his hand and bowing respectively, he said—'I have just come from the stable Mr. D'Aubrey, and thought you would like to know about the storm, sir.'

'What storm?' I exclaimed, 'oh, you mean the snow storm, yes—is it still snowing?' At that moment the window was crackling with the hail.

[24]

'Yes sir, and I thought I'd tell you that no one could come out to-night, for a horse without a wagon could not walk one hundred yards.'

'Thank you, Thomas, give the bay mare more corn to-morrow and call Henry.'—Henry, the waiter, came in expecting orders to put away the *clean* things and lock up for it was ten, and not a soul had arrived. 'Order supper Henry at eleven.'

'For whom, sir?'

'For me—what are you waiting for?'

'How much, sir,' said he, in a bewildered air. 'All of it.'

He looked anxious. He could not classify me, but discipline must be carried out, so Mary and I sat down to enough for twenty-five persons, who had never known the pangs of dyspepsia. As soon as we had finished I ordered a large portion of it down stairs, for the benefit of the servants and retired. They all looked pleased and I was satisfied. Mrs. Phillips had the nightmare at about two o'clock.

Before I took charge, the allies of my household were accustomed to come in at all hours and sit up till they were too sleepy to go to bed, looking the next morning like wet blotting paper. But that was soon stopped. For the morning of my address to them I stated that the house was shut up at ten p. m., and now and then it was amusing to hear the door open as the clock struck.

One night at about twelve as I was sitting at my desk in the library, I heard someone trying to get in. I knew it was the waiter who had slipped out without leave, so I turned out the gas, put my head out of the window and said 'I know it must be a robber, for they are all in,' and seeing his form I fired off my revolver overhead.—No servant ever tried again to enter by stealing in after hours. When my sister kept house I suffered much for want of dishes during many days in the week.—There was very little variety.

[25]

Sundays we had only potatoes and cold meat.

'Why,' I asked.

'They must go to church, my dear brother.'

Mondays, one fry, not even a roast, it was washing day, all the heat must be turned off from the oven for the boiler.—The cook wouldn't have it roasted in front, the only true way.

So no dessert could be baked.

Tuesdays I could have no company for it was ironing day, and the irons filled up the range and nothing extra could be made. I submitted to my sister.

But now I had soup every day, and whenever I saw anything very good in market I ordered it home and had it cook[Pg 13]ed. Strange isn't it, with the same range and the same cook? Before my reign we could not breakfast till nine, the cook said that the milkman came so late. During my reign we breakfasted at eight punctually, for I suggested to her the propriety of rising at six instead of seven and letting him in on his first trip instead of taking the milk from him on his return. My sister was obliged to tell her two or three days before hand that she was going to have company, that she might have time to get everything ready for dinner. I frequently brought home two or three guests with fish and game in the same carriage and ordered it as the fourth course while partaking of soup. On one occasion I brought in partridges twenty minutes before dinner. I went down stairs knowing she would be roused this time, and flanked her by saying, 'Hannah, you won't have time to pick those birds, so just draw them and *skin* them. I want them roasted.' Before she recovered from her astonishment I had departed.

Whenever a quarrel down stairs took place I never interfered as long as they did not talk loud, but the next day if I noticed any one in the sulks or a tendency to let things go by, I had the furniture of one

[26]

room changed to another. This required 'all hands' to work together, and I made them fly round so, that when it was done they were only too happy to go to lunch and rest, and I could hear many a joke and pleasant laugh rise from the kitchen table.

One rainy evening, as my sister and myself were sitting in front of the wood fire, exactly two months since the famous contract, and very much in the same position, and talking over everything but it, a timid knock was heard. I said 'come in,' and Sabina entered, looking very healthy and neat—I cannot say pretty, though she had a good figure.

I never asked questions on these occasions. I always made it difficult for them to talk in this, to them, gloomy room.—They had to stumble through themselves.

'Can I speak to you, sir.'

'Certainly, Sabina—go on.'

'I have come to say, sir, that—that—I have came to say, sir, that'—a pause; she looked very guilty.

'That's right, Sabina; you have come to say that—I understand—but what have you come to say?'

'I have come to say, sir, that—I have come to go, sir!'

I controlled myself. She was an excellent chambermaid; understood my ways thoroughly; and did her work well; had always been respectful to *me*, and was very steady. It would be a great loss, butdiscipline must be preserved, and my mind was at once made up. My sister looked surprised and sorry right out.

'Well, Sabina, when do you wish to go.'

'On Saturday, sir.'

[27]

Oh how my sister wanted to speak, but I looked at the tin box that held the contract and she bit her lip.

'Very well, Sabina, you have a perfect right to go when and where you please, and I will take great pleasure in writing out an excellent character for you. Let me see, (looking at my account book) that is two weeks wages making $8. I never make presents, but as you are going here is a ten dollar bill. Where would you like[Pg 14] your trunk carried, tell me and I will send it by Thomas Saturday morning?'

'Oh! it isn't that, sir,' said she, 'but—but, sir,' with the tears flowing rapidly.

'Why, what is the matter, Sabina?' (the first question apart from business I had ever asked.)

'I don't want to leave you, sir.'

'Well, that is strange, then why do you?' (business question.)

'I'm going, sir—I'm going, sir, to—be—married!' and she burst into tears.

(I congratulated myself on being a bachelor, if conjugal affection produced such an effect.)

'Oh! that's it,' said I, dryly. 'Well I hope you will be happy.'

'But you've been so kind, sir, you—'

'There now stop, I have only tried to be just,' said I, looking exultingly at my smiling sister, who took off a little gold stud and gave it to her with many wishes of a happy life.

Everything went on regularly as clock-work. There was a place for everything, and everything in its place. When the bell rang during

[28]

dear Mary's sway, it continued to ring, and on one occasion, a friend met me in the street and said:

'Why William, have you moved?'

I replied no, that we were very comfortable where we were, 'why do you ask?'

'That's very strange,' said he, 'we called yesterday at one o'clock and rang for twenty minutes. No one coming we concluded you had left for Europe.'

'No,' I said, feeling rather confused, 'the waiter I believe is subject to sciatica. At times he is taken suddenly and cannot move, and the reason we did not hear the bell, (I looked away as I said so,) his cries of pain are such that you cannot hear yourself speak.'

Now the door is answered before the first ring stops sounding. For I arranged it so as to vibrate long enough to give a person time to go from any part of the house in exactly two minutes; and no man of the world rings oftener than once every three minutes. I would not have written all this but my blessed sister soon entirely followed out my reformation and is fairly convinced, as she says, that when a man sets about any matter, he is very thorough: clear headed; and, above all, not easily put down.

Oh! if all women thought so! eh, Mr. Caudle? I knew one learned gentleman who only desired peace and good food. His wife never allowed him to offer a suggestion. She called him a genius, and made him mind.

Formerly Mary rose thoughtful, with the pressure of business on her brain. At meals she was abstracted, often worried, and at all times the repository of domestic troubles. Her healthy organization was altogether too mesmerized by the petty warfare below stairs. She was never idle, and yet rarely accomplished anything for *herself*. Her position in the household might have been called that of grand

[29]

finisher. She planned work and waited for its completion in vain. Finally she would bring it into the library and stitch—stitch—all through the pleasant evenings. I knew this, for I laid a plan. One April I asked her to[Pg 15] work me a pair of slippers on cloth. I presume a clever woman, undisturbed, could have delivered them over to me at the end of the week. Now, no one is more clever than my sister; yet I did not get those slippers till December; and then she handed them to me in sadness, and said, with an attempt at cheerfulness, 'dear William, I worked one myself, but my duties are such that I gave out the other to that poor woman whose husband is at sea. Has'nt she done it well?' Now, I find her reading, paying visits, and often of an evening she comes to me and says, 'William, would'nt you like some new handkerchiefs embroidered?' or 'can't I mend anything for you? I have just finished my music and have nothing to do.'

On another occasion, while she was mending—not making reader—but *mending*, her children's clothes, I offered to read one of Ik Marvel's reveries of a bachelor, a special favorite of mine. She thanked me, and I proceeded. On finishing one of his admirable paragraphs, I put the book down and exclaimed, 'isn't that capital?'

She said at once, 'no, I think it is very discouraging.'

'Discouraging! Why, what in the world do you mean, Mary?"

'Excuse me, William, but I was'nt listening. The fact of it is, there has been another row down stairs, and I do think that girl ought to be ashamed of herself to treat Susan so;' and then for *one*hour a topographical and analytical history of the entire household was gone into, with a *con amore* spirit, which lasted through two segars and a glass of water. I never spoke. On these occasions they don't want you to talk; only to listen. They say in a sweet and confiding manner, 'you know I have no one to sympathize with me;' and off they go, like the recitation of Pope's Homer, made by some school girl who has been sentenced to run through so many lines. I slipped the reveries into their place, so that she would not be hurt, and I do assure you that when she had got through I believe if you had asked her suddenly 'who discovered America?' she would have replied 'An Irishman—I forget his name.'

Formerly there was ever a business gravity about her: now she always appeared with a sweet smile that lit up her countenance, as though it had been sprinkled all over with sun-powder.

Difficult indeed was it for Mary to order anything without an advance notice, for otherwise she was forced to start her little bark through the Scylla and Charybdis of 'fire island,' namely, 'The fire's too low, marm;' or 'I've just put on coal, marm.'

Now she reads to me herself, and marks the prettiest passages in Tennyson, which no woman could find out if her understanding had been mortgaged by servants.

Before, no matter what dish of meat was set before me, it was always *dry*, or the gravy made of butter and *water*. I have often seen mutton chops come on table looking like little islands of meat surrounded by water, on which might be detected a tickley benders of grease. Five minutes conversation on my part supplied the deficiency, and caused one can of lard to outlast six of those in olden times.[Pg 16]

When I first took charge of the kitchen, the cook made one struggle—but only one. The reply to her question indicated such ignorance or indifference on my part, that everything suggested in future was served as directed, and well done. Having ordered many dishes one day—I don't know whether it was washing or ironing day, I never used to ask: I also gave the ingredients of a very nice pudding, and said 'can you make that?'

'I know how, sir, but can't to-day.'

'Why not?'

[31]

'There is no room in the oven, you have filled it with your orders, and it is impossible to bake it this afternoon.'

'You cannot bake it, then?'

'No, sir.'

'Then *broil* it!'

End of the book.